# 12 CHRISTMAS PROCESSIONALS

Andrew Fletcher, Andrew Gant, Colin Hand, Richard Lloyd
Colin Mawby, Dom Andrew Moore, Philip Moore
June Nixon, Noel Rawsthorne, Richard Shephard
Christopher Tambling, Quentin Thomas

Kevin Mayhew

We hope you enjoy the music in *12 Christmas Processionals*.
Further copies of this are available from
your local music shop or Christian bookshop.

In case of difficulty, please contact the publisher direct by writing to:

The Sales Department
KEVIN MAYHEW LTD
Rattlesden
Bury St Edmunds
Suffolk IP30 0SZ

Phone 01449 737978
Fax 01449 737834

Please ask for our complete catalogue of outstanding Church Music.

Front Cover: *A Procession in Winter* by Giacomo di Chiroco (1845-1884)
Reproduced by kind permission of Fine Art Photographic Library, London.

Cover design by Veronica Ward and Graham Johnstone

First published in Great Britain in 1995 by Kevin Mayhew Ltd

ISBN 0 86209 686 3
Catalogue No:1400054

Music Editor: Tamzin Howard
Music setting by Louise Hill

Printed and bound in Great Britain

# Contents

# INTRADA: UNTO US IS BORN A SON

Andrew Fletcher

a tempo

ff + Reed

# CHRISTMAS SCHERZO

June Nixon

rit.     a tempo

Solo

– Gt. to Ped.

Solo

+ Gt. to Ped.

10

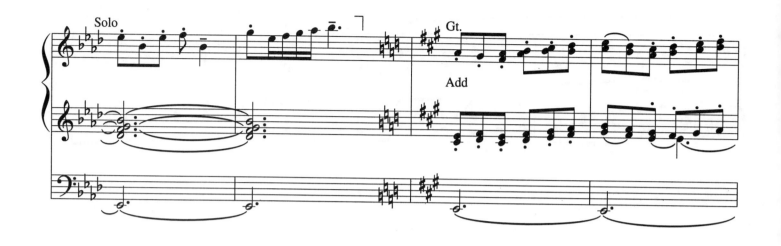

# TOCCATA-NOEL

## Christopher Tambling

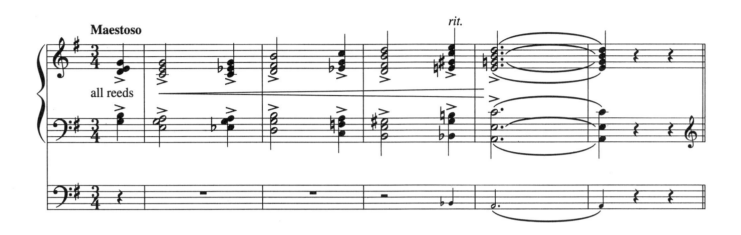

# THE HOLLY AND THE IVY

Richard Shephard

# ALL THE BELLS ON EARTH

## Colin Hand

23

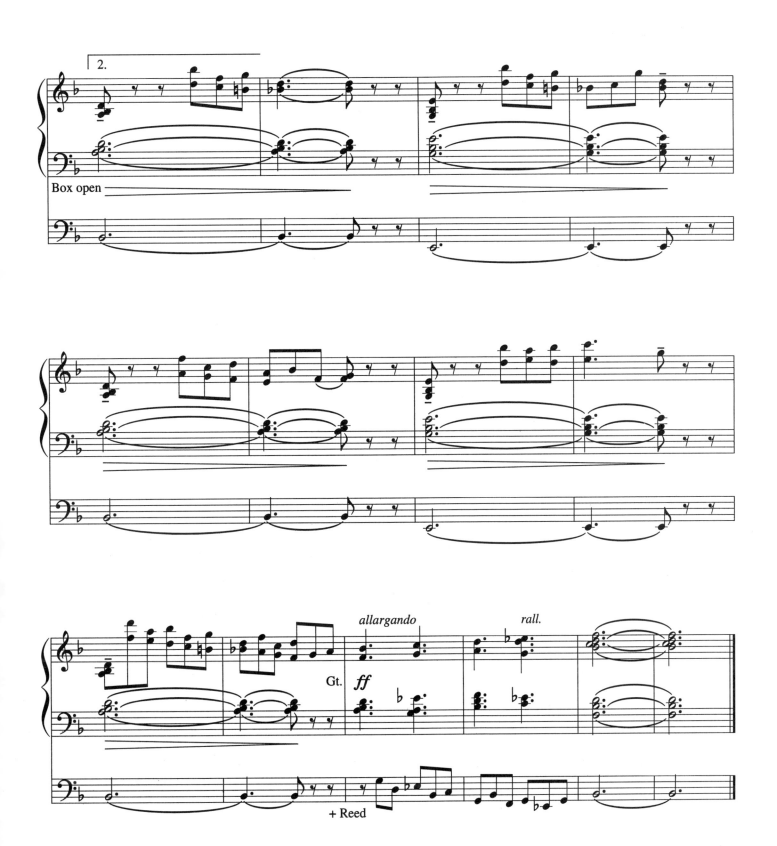

# IT CAME UPON THE MIDNIGHT CLEAR

Colin Mawby

# CHRISTMAS PRELUDE

Andrew Gant

# DIVINUM MYSTERIUM

## Noel Rawsthorne

* Optional repeat

# CHRISTMAS PROCESSIONAL

## Philip Moore

**Moderato maestoso** ($\quad$ = c.76)

# IMPROVISATION ON THE TWELVE TUNES OF CHRISTMAS

Dom Andrew Moore

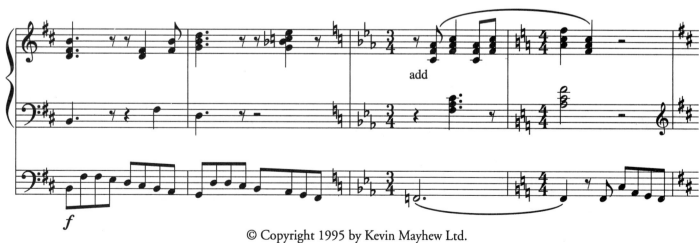

molto rit.

cresc.

add

Allegro
Gt.

Tuba *f*

*f*

43

# A PARTRIDGE IN A PEAR TREE

Quentin Thomas

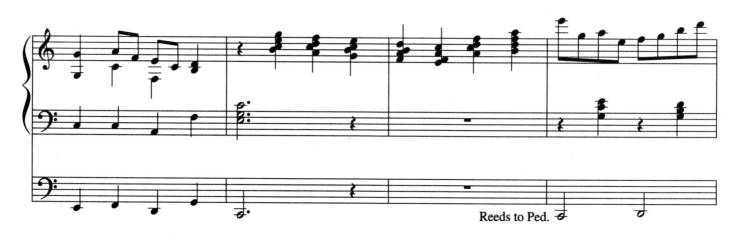

Reeds to Ped.

– Reeds

*rall.*

**Lento**

a tempo

ff stringendo

48

Full    *ff* *emphatico e risoluto*

\+ Reeds *ff*

**Cheekily**

# CHRISTMAS POSTLUDE

Richard Lloyd

*2nd time to Coda* ⊕

51

**⊕ CODA**

*molto allargando*     *lento*     *a tempo*

*allargando*     *più lento*     *rall.*

# About the Composers

**Andrew Fletcher** (*b.*1950) is a teacher, composer, accompanist and recitalist, performing regularly all over the world.

**Andrew Gant** (*b.*1963) is Director of Music in Chapel at Selwyn College, Cambridge. He also directs the *Light Blues* vocal ensemble and is Musical Director of the Thursford Christmas concerts. He has worked extensively as an arranger for both radio and television.

**Colin Hand** (*b.*1929) is a composer of choral, orchestral and chamber music for both professional and amateur players.

**Richard Lloyd** (*b.*1933) was Assistant Organist of Salisbury Cathedral and successively Organist of Hereford and Durham Cathedrals. He now divides his time between examining and composing.

**Colin Mawby** (*b.*1936) composes in many forms. He was previously Choral Director at Radio Telefís Éireann, the national broadcasting authority in the Republic of Ireland, and Master of the Music at Westminster Cathedral.

**Dom Andrew Moore** (*b.*1954) is a Benedictine Monk at Downside Abbey, near Bath.

**Philip Moore** (*b.*1943) is Organist and Master of the Music at York Minster.

**June Nixon** is Organist and Director of the Choir at St Paul's Cathedral, Melbourne, Australia. She also teaches at the Melbourne University School of Music.

**Noel Rawsthorne** (*b.*1929) was Organist of Liverpool Cathedral for twenty-five years and City Organist and Artistic Director at St George's Hall, Liverpool. He was also Senior Lecturer in Music at St Katharine's College Liverpool until his retirement in 1993.

**Richard Shephard** (*b.*1949) is Headmaster of the Minster School, York and Vicar Choral in York Minster. He has served on the Archbishops' Commission on Church Music and on Church Music Commissions on Cathedrals.

**Christopher Tambling** (*b.*1964) is the Director of Music at Glenalmond College in Perthshire.

**Quentin Thomas** (*b.*1972) is a member of the teaching staff at the Oratory School, Woodcote, Berkshire. He is also active as a conductor, performer and composer.